Deer

Nature's *Timid* but *Elegant*

Dr. Richard A. NeSmith

Love of Nature Series

ISSUE 25

Applied Principles of Education & Learning

APE-Learning

© 2020 Richard A. NeSmith
Love of Nature Series

All Rights Reserved.

No part of this book may be reproduced, transmitted, or stored in any form or by any means except for your own personal use without the author's express, written permission. All graphs, drawings, and charts are created by the author or utilize public illustrations according to fair use for teaching, research, scholarship, and reporting. Some photos are those of the authors, and some are Creative Commons licensed. Special thanks to the following who contributed pro bono from their collections.[i] Thank you all.

This book contains material used under the "Fair Use" of copyrighted material as provided for in section 107 of the U.S. Copyright Law. Every attempt has been made to provide credit to outside organizations or individuals who have provided images, illustrations, documents, or other information.

dr.nesmith@gmail.com

http://richardnesmith.obior.cc

All images in this book are copyrighted by their respective photographers.

JUNE 2025

ISBN: 9798580163604

FLESCH-KINCAID GRADE LEVEL: 8.6

Deer: Nature's Timid but Elegant
(Family: Cervidae)

Deer are iconic symbols in North America. They represent strength, grace, agility, and elegance. Deer have even become icons of insurance corporations and other large companies as their emblem or brand. It was deer that became the American staple in the early days of

colonization and westward expansion. Deer are, in many ways, foundational. In American history, many families only survived during times of hardships because of the availability and capability to put deer and turkey on the dinner table.

All deer are cloven-hooved animals belonging to the same Order[1] and are described as ***ungulate*** animals. Of these, the Class **Cervidae** is a *true deer* family that is antlered, hoofed **ruminants**. There are 47 species, comprised of over 60 different **subspecies** of deer worldwide. This group includes three subfamilies[2]: brocket deer, caribou, ***deer***, moose, and relatives. From these, we will focus on the six species living in North America that tend to have a smaller body size and frame.

❶ **White-tail Deer** ❹ **Mule Deer**

❷ **Black-tail Deer** ❺ **Key Deer**

❸ **Fallow Deer** ❻ **Axis Deer**

In future issues of *Love of Nature,* we will address other larger members of the deer family, such as the caribou, pronghorn deer, elk, and moose.

Range

White-tail deer live in most of North America except Alaska, Hawaii, and parts of the Southwest. Mule deer range from the Great Plains to the Western coastal ranges and from the Yukon Territory to Sonora and Baja Mexico. Black-tail deer are found in western Oregon from the Coast

---

[1] Artiodactyla - meaning even-toed
[2] Capriolinae

Range east to the Cascade Mountains. Key deer are restricted to a small area in the Florida Keys, and a few other introduced isolated localities. The Fallow deer and Axis deer are also introduced exotic species and generally are found in remote, specific regions. We will find that these graceful animals are usually **timid but elegant creatures** to watch and admire.

Characteristics

All deer in the Family Cervidae (pronounced ser-vih-day) are **herbivorous** (plant-eaters), hoofed, warm-blooded mammals whose antlers shed annually. Male deer (stag[3] or **buck**) tend to be larger (**sexual dimorphism**) than the female (called a **doe** or hind). The offspring is called a **fawn**, kid, or calf. Those juvenile deer not yet mature (one to two years of age) are called **yearlings**. Yearling males just obtaining their antlers are called *button bucks*.

---

[3] Some reserve the term "stag" for the largest of bucks.

Deer tend to have long, powerful legs, a small tail, and long ears. Deer come in a wide range of sizes. Of these focused on in this book, the mule deer are generally the larger species and tend to have similar sized animals across the regions. Black-tail deer, a **subspecies** of the mule deer, are slightly smaller than their close cousins. White-tail deer vary in size based on their environment. Fallow deer seem to be in the medium range, while the Key and Axis deer are the smallest.

Antler growth is an annual cycle in a male deer (**buck**), which grows and are then shed. Antlers are the fastest growing bone known to date. Most males have antlers, which grow from boney supporting structures on the upper forehead called **pedicels**, the growing base attached to the skull.

Males typically begin developing a new set of antlers in late spring, just before the breeding season. This timing ensures that males have strong, hardened antlers for fighting competitions with other males when establishing dominance and breeding privileges. Antler growth is controlled by hormones regulated by the *length of the day* (called **photoperiod**), which affects the **pineal gland** deep in the brain.[4] Antler growth is an expensive biological investment and requires large amounts of nutrients and energy.

As the days lengthen in sunlight following winter, there is a

---

[4] Located in the brain, the pineal gland detects changes in day length, or photoperiod. This gland affects the pituitary gland to produce hormones that control not only antler growth, shedding of velvet and the hardening of the antlers, but also male and female reproductive cycling.

reduction in **melatonin**, which initiates the hormone cycle responsible for starting antler growth. New antler growth is covered in a hair-like membrane (a skin covering) called "velvet," which is rich in nerves and blood vessels[5] throughout late spring and summer. Deer in this state have

---

[5] The velvet skin is a living tissue actively pumping/supplying blood to the bone cells in the growing antlers.

antlers that look spongy or hairy-like and are said to be *in velvet.*

While antlers are *in velvet*, they are sensitive to touch (and pain). They are subject to injury, cuts, and bruises, resulting in deformed antlers.[6] During this stage, bucks will venture more out of the woods and thickets to open grasslands to avoid injuring or irritating their sensitive and growing antlers. In well-nourished deer, antler growth by early summer can reach one inch per day.

As antlers grow, they are very high in water content and low in *dry matter* content (about 80%).[7] Dry matter includes calcium and phosphorus.[8] By August, antler growth slows down and begins to harden (*mineralize*). In late August or early September,

---

[6] Antler deformations can also be caused by leg injuries, which often result from deer-vehicle accidents.

[7] Velvet antlers are composed of proteins, amino acids, minerals, lipids and water. Specific key compounds that have been identified in deer antler include collagen, glucosamine sulfate, chondroitin sulfate and growth factors that aid in cartilage cell development.

[8] Males with diets low in calcium and phosphorus often have delayed antler growth and velvet shedding.

the buck's biology changes and testosterone increases, and antler growth stops. Blood ceases to flow to the antlers, causing a grayish color and initiating the velvet skin's cracking, drying out, and dying.

The velvet skin then sheds (called *velvet peel*), begins within 24 hours, and falls off within one to three days.[9] Still, the deer will accelerate the process by rubbing it off against trees, shrubs, or other vegetation, including tall grass. Some have reported this to appear as a stressful time for bucks and one that can consume their attention. The antlers become calcified and hardened. This rubbing will result in polished, hard antlers during the breeding season.

Healthy bucks will maintain their hardened antlers throughout the breeding season; however, the chemical composition changes. Hardened antlers are high in dry

---

[9] Some have observed deer eating the velvet skin, which would not be entirely unusual as many animals often eat products made by their own body, including the placenta, mucous covering, or old discarded chitin body shells.

matter and low in water (60% ash and 40% protein). From
the antler's tip toward the base, the ash content increases,

and lipid (fats and oils), and protein contents decrease.

As antlers mature, the ash and some mineral contents increase, and moisture content decreases. Though variation occurs, males will shed their antlers (called *antler-drop*) in late December to early March. As soon as the antlers are shed, it will immediately trigger the melatonin's hormonal action and the pedicels. When it does, it starts the process all over again during the new season. Growth will become apparent within several weeks. Discovering shed antlers is a rare find as they have a high content of protein and calcium phosphate and, as a result, are consumed quickly by rodents.[10]

A **beam** is a word used to describe the left and right main prominent antlers from which others grow. The two main antler beams curve forward without dividing or branching. A branched antler is called a rack. As a deer matures, it grows more points or tips (called **tines**) on the antler beam.

A "point" is a growing branch of a deer antler that measures at least one inch in length. These eventually reach a maximum number and become smaller year after year as the deer ages. Antler development reaches optimum in the fifth and sixth years of age.

---

[10] Hardened antlers are composed of about 22 percent calcium and 11 percent phosphorus. These are consumed rather quickly by squirrels, chipmunks, groundhogs, and mice.

Yearling deer typically produce antlers called **spikes**. These are two hardened antlers that do not branch or fork. However, older nutritionally challenged bucks can also be restricted to the spike formation.[11] There is a misnomer

often shared that tries to relate a buck deer's age to his antlers. It is true that as a buck ages, his antlers will become heavier and better developed. However, *there is no precise way to accurately determine a deer's age other than looking at the teeth.* Despite the many stories hunters tell each other, the size of the antlers and the number of points on the antlers is not a reliable age guide. ***Antler size is more a***

---

[11] Wildlife management experts hold that when spikes represent more than 25 percent of yearling bucks, it usually indicates too many deer are present for the available resources.

function of diet and heredity than it is of age.[12] On average, males increase their antler size until 6.5 years of age, when antler growth is maximized.

<hr>

[12] The University of Missouri reported: "A difference of 8 percent and 16 percent protein in a deer's diet at 4 years of age can cause a 20-inch difference in antler size." See: https://bit.ly/3a04YbQ

Deer range in color from dark to very light brown, and fawns are born with white spots to help camouflage them from predators. These spots disappear within three to four months, usually with their new winter coat. The oldest known deer in the wild lived for 20 years, but few deer live past 10 years of age. A deer may live for 11 to 12 years (**lifespan**). However, most die long before then due to predators, hunters, malnutrition, disease, or collisions with automobiles.

Diet

Deer are **herbivorous** mammals that eat only vegetation and **ruminate**. Ruminating occurs as the deer brings the food back up into their mouth from the first stomach chamber and continues chewing it. This process is called *chewing the **cud***. **Mastication**, the *chewing, grinding,* and *crushing* of food with the teeth, increases the surface area of the plants eaten and mechanically breaks up indigestible cellulose fibers into small bits, pieces, and particles. Larger surface areas[13] enhance microbial (chemical) digestion, speeding up the **fermenting** of cellulose in a specialized stomach before actual digestion occurs. These gut **microbes** can release **nutrition** for the animal that would not be available otherwise.

A ruminant's stomach is a multi-chambered organ. It is usually composed of four separate chambers. This system allows the digestion of large quantities of plant matter that would be relatively indigestible for most other types of

---

13 Called the surface-to-volume ratio.

mammals, mainly grass and leaves. The first chamber, called the **rumen**, is for storage. The rumen is slightly centered on the animal's left side. It is the largest stomach compartment and contains several sacs. Depending on the species, it can hold 15-25 gallons or more of partially-chewed plant material.[14] It acts as a storage tank for food but mainly serves as a fermentation vat.[15]

Here microscopic bacteria and other microorganisms (all collectively called **microbes**) live, grow, and reproduce. These microbes are capable of breaking down plant matter called **cellulose**. They also produce several by-products, such as unstable fatty acids, which the animal absorbs and uses as energy. Breaking down degradable protein produces

---

[14] Approximately 6-10 lbs. (2.8-4.6 kg) of grasses.
[15] Its internal surface is covered with tiny projections called papillae, which increase the surface area of the rumen and allow better absorption of digested nutrients.

amino acids and ammonia. The former is a valuable

Axis Deer.

requirement for life, while the latter is: ❶ a significant source of nitrogen[16] for microbial growth and ❷ a waste product for the animal.

Though they have no upper incisor teeth, deer all use their

---

[16] The microbes also convert non-protein nitrogen to ammonia.

Axis male buck.

molars to chew their **cud**. The cud is partially digested food returned from their first stomach to the mouth for further chewing. They have three other "false" stomachs. After a deer fills its **paunch** (gut), it lies down to rest and will chew its cud. After chewing its cud for a time, the deer re-swallows the food. It passes into the second portion of the stomach. After about 16 hours, food passes to the third chamber and then on into the small intestines.

The benefit for deer (and herbivores such as cows) is that they can gather a great deal of food in a very short time and digest it later. On average, a deer can eat anywhere from 6% to 8% of its body weight every day. Depending on size, this can amount to six to eight pounds of grass, hay, leaves, and acorns for a 100-pound deer. The main disadvantage of herbivores is the low amount of nutrition obtained from plants. Then there is the time factor needed to digest plants. Deer, however, can feed often or continually.

Deer may travel from one mile or more to graze on grass. But much more territory may be required during winter when food options are limited. Diet and seasons are closely linked. For example, scarce food in winter may cause deer to seek out more nuts (such as pecans, hickory nuts, and beechnuts) and acorns than during the greener seasons.

Key deer - buck.

In fall, deer will be more active when preparing for the winter season by grazing more frequently and for longer periods to put on weight than during the coming cold season. Different plants, and different parts of plants, do not provide the same level of nutrition. Deer have food preferences and often select the growing tips of plants to browse. The tips typically are succulent and the most nutrient-rich portion.

Deer recognize these nutritional differences and try to eat

accordingly. For example, a few studies had indicated that deer preferred natural vegetation over a nutritionally complete deer pellet ration in spring when new leaves emerged. During late summer and early fall, these food choices are vital. The body-to-fat ratio is critical for survival but also determines the potential for reproduction during the mating season. Diet even affects the growth and timing of antlers. Undernourished males produced only spike antlers at 2.5 years of age. In contrast, adequately nourished males can produce at least 6 points at the same age.[17]

Spring brings new life from new plant growth and offspring. In the winter months, deer tend to change become less active. They become more active in spring and return to being foraging during the twilight hours. Though deer typically are active throughout the day, they are most active at dusk and dawn (**crepuscular**). They spend most of their day foraging for food and part of it bedding down in familiar and comfortable locations.

---

[17] Some yearling specimens have been found that ranged in size from spikes to 10 or more antler points.

Spring brings some of the deer's favorite foods: fields of alfalfa and clover grasses. Besides, they enjoy grasses, which make up almost nine percent of their diet. These include rescuegrass (sometimes called bunchgrass), wintergrass (a type of ryegrass), witchgrass, panic grasses (sometimes called cereal grasses), sedges, rushes, and wild and cultivated rye oats. White-tailed deer prefer forbs (herbaceous flowering plants) when they are available.

Though a smorgasbord of fresh delights, they also like to eat weedy plants, including dandelions. Other enjoyables include berries (blueberries and blackberries), ragweed, asters, fungi, and vines, including grape and honeysuckle. In eastern forests, buds and twigs of maple, sassafras, poplar, aspen, and birch trees are consumed, and many shrubs.

As summer approaches, fruits begin to ripen. By late summer and fall, deer delight in low-hanging crab apples, persimmons, and pears. Autumn ryegrasses, corn, and wheat become food staples as they start to prepare for the winter months again. Deer always welcome vegetable gardens. Of course, the deer are not always so welcomed by the growers or farmers. Winter can be challenging, if not brutal, as most leaves and green plants have died or fallen

During early spring bucks begin to shed their antlers.

from trees. This scarcity of living plants makes woody stems, twigs, bark, shoots, and the bud-tips of the branches of oaks, red cedar, and willow trees a means of survival. Conifers are often eaten in winter when other plants become scarce.[18]

---

[18] Not a choice food because conifers/pines have less phosphorus accessible in those acidic soils (low in pH).

Habitats

As with all mammals and most animals, what is needed for survival is simply food, water[19], shelter, and space to move about to find daily requirements. These are the essential components of a **habitat**. Habitat is defined as the collection of resources, the physical and the biological factors, present in an area that enable the survival and reproduction of a particular species. A habitat is only as good as the quality, quantity, and availability of food. Forests of different ages support different numbers of deer. Deer density and **carrying capacity** both address the number of deer that could be supported in an environment.

Axis deer herd.

Both are directly related to the habitat and depend on the

---

[19] Deer drink about 3 to 6 quarts of water per day.

ecosystem's heartiness.

Deer are rather adaptable. They are found in a variety of different ecosystems. They live in wetlands, deciduous forests, grasslands, rainforests, arid scrublands, mountains, and even deserts. Habitat loss or encroachment can affect

deer health and populations. Deer have been found to live in suburban and urban settings, and they are often seen on

Key deer (buck).

or around golf courses. They are best suited to forested habitats. Woodlands and timberlands provide deer with a place to eat, rest, escape, bear, and rear young.

In focusing more closely on the six North American deer,

we consider a few specific characteristics.

WHITE-TAIL DEER (Odocoileus *virginianus*)

The white-tailed deer is the most abundant deer in the United States. White-tail deer are some of the most timid of all deer. The white-tail deer, also known as the Virginia white-tail, is precisely as the name implies, originating from the flashy white-tail most seen as they run for cover. The tail can look much longer, pure white, and waving like a flag in the air when this deer is alarmed. This species of deer tends to be smaller in comparison to the mule deer.

Flagging of the tail and the origin of the name "white-tail" deer.

More than the others focused on here, White-tail deer have the most extensive ranges in size differences across the diverse regions. Although fully mature males can weigh 300 pounds (136.8 kg), most white-tale males weigh 150 to 175 pounds (68.0 to 79.8 kg), and females usually weigh around 100 pounds (45.4 kg). The adult white-tailed deer has a bright, reddish-brown summer coat and a duller grayish-brown winter coat. White fur is located in a band behind the nose, in circles around the eyes, inside the ears, over the chin and throat, on the legs' upper insides, and beneath the tail. The **fawns** have reddish coats with white spots and tend to camouflage nicely, especially blending into grassy areas. About 20-30% of fawns will die during their first year.

MULE DEER (Odocoileus *hemionus*)

These deer are found west of the Missouri River, especially in the Rocky Mountain region of North America. The mule deer is unique. It has a black-tipped tail and **bifurcated**[20] antlers that fork as they grow instead of branching from a single main beam.

Although a strong deer and quite capable of running, mule deer tend to be observed *stotting* (also called pronking)[21] with all four feet coming down together. It is believed that a mule deer stott as a slower means of escape than to just galloped away.

---

[20] divided into two branches or forks
[21] Tend to spring or bounce into the air, lifting all four feet off the ground simultaneously. Usually, the legs are held in a relatively stiff position.

Adult mule deer usually reach 121-331 lbs. (55-150 kg), though some "trophy" specimens have been found to get 460 lbs. (210 kg). Like most deer, the doe is smaller than the buck and averages 95 to 198 lbs. (43 to 90 kg), with an average of 150 lbs. (68 kg). Some cross-breeding does occur between the mule deer and the white-tail.[22]

BLACK-TAIL DEER (Odocoileus *hemionus columbianus*)

Black-tails are a subspecies of mule deer found in western Oregon from the Coast Range east to the Cascade Mountains. They are an **edge-adapted species** using the region's dense forest cover to hide during the day and more open early successional forest to feed at dawn and dusk.[23]

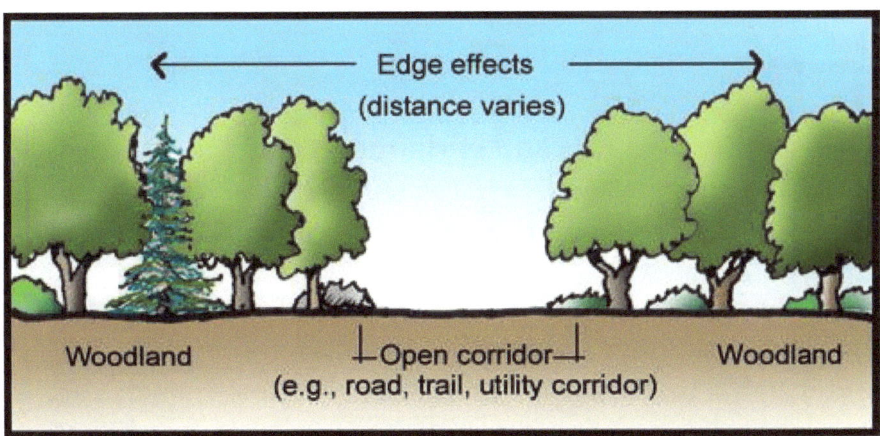

Edge effect: Require some adaptations for survival, creating edge-adapted species.

KEY DEER (Odocoileus *virginianus clavium*)

---

22 Whitetail bucks will breed with mule deer does, but the offspring usually retain the white-tail characteristics. Reverse mating — mule deer bucks to white-tail does — is rarer. Where the two species share a common range, the white-tail tends to dominate.

23 Where two ecosystems join or overlap is called an ecotone. In these areas, an edge effect occurs, referring to the changes in population or community structures that occur at the boundary of two habitats. This is called edge effect. Here a larger number of animals may live between the two zones and as a result the species here must adapt to different circumstances then in either habitat.

Fallow deer.

The Key deer is a rare and **endangered** deer that lives only in the Florida Keys and is the smallest of the 28 subspecies of Virginia white-tailed deer (O. virginianus).

These are the smallest North American deer. The largest males typically stand only about 1 meter at the shoulder and weigh a maximum of around 80-100 lbs. Females are smaller, weighing 65 pounds on average. Key deer fawns are about the size of a small housecat. They seem to have adapted well to a salt-tolerant subtropical climate. This climate allows them to reproduce during any time of the year; however, the fawning peak occurs during the spring and summer months.

According to the U.S. Fish and Wildlife Service, only about 700 to 800 are found in the entire state. The Big Pine Key and No Name Key populations are estimated to be 600, with another 100 to 200 on other Lower Keys and Backcountry islands. It is recorded that the number of Key deer in 1957 may have reached a low of 27. Their range in the last 100 years has shrunk from 60 linear miles to 6 miles.

Fallow deer.

Like most deer, Key deer are most active at dusk and dawn. They tend to remain within the limits of the cool pine rocklands during the heat of the day. The two endangering issues for Key deer at present are habitat loss and habituation to humans feeding them. Unfortunately, people illegally feed them on roadsides as the deer have learned to solicit handouts. Feeding these deer is illegal but difficult to control as the deer forage on the sides of most roads, eagerly approaching slow-moving drivers for food. Unfortunately, over-familiarization with roads and automobiles causes many to be killed each year by traffic.

Axis deer herd.

In addition, concentrated deer populations facilitate the spreading of parasites (ticks and mites) and disease.

FALLOW DEER (Odocoileus *dama dama*)

Fallow deer is a small European deer, named after its color (*dama*, pale brown), though colors vary, including white and black. They are considered *ornamental* species due to their size, color, and cuteness. They are considered one of the most beautiful deer. They tend to be very popular and are often found in wildlife parks and zoos. Escapees have been found in the wild. The fallow deer's most distinctive feature is the bucks' beautiful flattened antlers, powerful short legs, and extremely fast. Fallow deer have a natural resistance to many diseases and parasites.

These deer were introduced to parts of North America and are inclined to be shy and withdrawn in the forests. A small feral population is found on one barrier island in Georgia.

Another isolated population lives in Texas, where they are hunted on large game ranches. Fallow deer thrive on any pasture that would support cattle, and consequently, are raised as livestock in Pennsylvania. Some feral fallow deer have been reported in Indiana. Small breeding populations have been identified near Argonne National Laboratories in northeastern Illinois and on the isolated Belle Isle (Detroit,

Axis deer.

Michigan). Other small groups have also been noted in western Kentucky and Tennessee.

AXIS DEER (Odocoileus *hemionus*)

Axis deer, also called the Chital or spotted deer, were introduced from India as a game species to Texas in 1932. In 1988, self-sustaining herds were found in 27 U.S. counties located in Central and South Texas. The deer are most populated on the Edwards Plateau, where the land is similar to their native India. These species seem to be favored by rifle hunters year-round as for trophy hunting that can be enjoyed anytime one desires to hunt.

Behavior

Deer are very social and travel in groups called **herds**. A dominant male often leads and watches over a female herd or a herd of males. In other situations, a dominant female will lead her own female herd. Some herds can have vast numbers of members. However, the group dynamics change during breeding (**rutting**) season.

By August, about the time the antlers have hardened, a dramatic change occurs in male behavior. The male

Axis doe.

"buddy" groups that traveled and foraged together now change dynamics and competition emerges. Bucks begin to knock heads, and with the "rut" season entering, hormones and pheromones start to cause the deer to stake out a territory. During the breeding season, male deer use their

antlers to fight and establish dominance over other male deer. Bucks will often lock antlers and push one another to determine which individual is more assertive, stronger, and muscular, showing a dominance hierarchy between individual animals.[24] Bucks begin to separate into their own

---

[24] However, current research does not substantiate antler size correlating with dominance between individual white-tailed deer. Larger antlers do not make one the leader. See: https://bit.ly/3a04YbQ

domains. Scuffles and fights determine dominance and breeding rights. A similar response occurs among the female deer clans.

Eyes

Deer see very well, but their vision is much better in low light than during daylight hours. Deer have very wide eyes and take in plenty of light to see their paths to favorite food sources, monitor the environment, and avoid danger or predation. With horizontally-shaped pupils, deer pupils are three times larger than our round pupils. This difference enables them to gather *nine times more light* than we can. Also, their eyes function exceptionally well in low light. This is because a deer's **retina** contains 20 times more **rods** than cones. Rods enable low light (*black and white* *vision*). **Cones** enable **color** *vision*.[25] Their night vision is estimated to be at least 18 times greater than humans.

Like humans, the rods dominate the deer's vision in low-light or dark conditions, restricting its ability to detect colors. They leave the safety of vegetation to search for food more often in the low-light hours than at any other time during the day. A human's vision (**visual acuity**) is that of 20-20.[26] It is estimated that a deer's visual acuity is between 20-60 to 20-100. This data suggests that overall, a deer's vision is nearly three times worse than an average human's sight. Namely, this indicates that we see more details than a deer would, but that might not be an advantage

[25] The study of color vision in deer is still relatively new and not fully understood. There are suggestions that deer see blues up to 20 times better than humans can. On another note, there is evidence that deer's perceptions of light reflections may actually be more important and useful than camouflage clothing.

[26] This is defined as a person reading an eye chart sees the same line of letters at 20 feet that people with normal vision see at 20 feet.

for deer survival. *Deer are better at seeing movement than stationary objects.*[27] Recently, during an early morning hike, this author encountered a healthy spike deer (a yearling with unbranched antlers on both sides). Staying completely still not only made it difficult for him to identify me but also stimulated his interest. This young buck slowly ventured his way up towards me to about 30 feet, trying to decide who or what I was (see photo below). After six or

seven minutes, he decided he had seen enough and slowly reentered the bush.

On the back of the eye membrane, the retina has a mirror-like layer called the **tapetum lucidum**. When shining a light at a deer at night, one gets a reflection called eyeshine, which appears as a glow. Those bright eyes are the tapetum lucidum reflecting light. Upon entering the deer's eyes, light washes across the millions of rods in their retinas. The light then *flows back* across them a second time after bouncing off the tapetum lucidum, doubling the eye's amount of usable light. The eyeshine of a deer is usually whitish but

---

[27] This tends to be true of the majority of animals, and especially mammals.

can also appear light green or yellowish.

Another interesting note is that of light-spectrum and how well deer see reflected light. When deer flee threats with their white tail flagging, we have learned that they're waving powerful visual cues to other deer. In addition to excellent sight, deer process what they see about 2.5 times faster than humans in low light and twice as fast in daylight.

Ears

Deer and humans appear to detect sounds of low-to-moderate frequency at about the same intensity. However, deer hear the high frequencies much better.[28] For example, a cat can hear much fainter sounds than either the deer or humans across a wide range of frequencies. This research all seems to indicate that a deer's hearing is not more acute than our own.

---

[28] Interesting enough, the "deer whistles" once placed on car bumpers to help avoid deer-car collisions have since been found to be useless because the high frequencies produced appear to be out of the hearing range of deer.

Nose

Though sight and hearing are essential senses for survival, they often are not the first indicators of potential danger or predators. Researchers have found that a deer's sense of

smell, like a dog's, can be anywhere from 500 to 1,000 times more acute than a human's smell. Further, scientists say that white-tails have thousands of sensitive receptors in their nostrils, which they use to sort out up to six scents at one time. A deer can pick up a hiker's smell one-half mile away.

Spooked deer will return to their bedding area, but the amount of time greatly depends on how much the intrusion frightened them. Even a threat that is only recognized by its smell in the wind can set the deer on edge and cause it to become overly cautious. Seeing a threat will keep a deer away for longer than if it just smelled a predator. However,

the sense of smell is so acute that it explains why those hiking downwind seldom see deer.[29]

Reproduction

When deer breed is dependent on where it lives. This period

---

[29] Hiking with the wind to one's face often results in seeing a greater variety of wildlife.

is commonly referred to as the **rutting** season and typically occurs between the middle of October to early December when deer mate. More specifically, deer in mild climate areas breed during late autumn or early winter. Deer living in lower latitudes mate from late spring into early summer. Deer that live in tropical climates mate whenever they want which could be several times per year.

Deer carry their young for a gestation period of 180 to 240 days. For northern and southern white-tailed deer,

gestation is around 193 to 205 days. Usually, the larger the deer, the longer the mother carries it in her womb. Deer usually only have one to three **fawns**. Fawns are weaned around two to five months, and maturation (ability to bear offspring) is species-specific and limited to reaching a certain size. Upon birth, a fawn is up and walking within the first 20 minutes.

Miscellaneous

Deer can sprint as fast as 35 miles per hour (56.3 kph) but cannot maintain that speed for long periods of time. They are also exceptional at jumping and leaping. *An adult deer can clear a seven-foot* (2.1 m) *fence from a standing position* and 10 feet while running. It can cover as much as 30 feet (9.1 m) in a single leap while running.

White-tail deer are good swimmers and will use large

Buck scraping and rubbing off the velvet membrane.

Button buck.

streams and lakes to escape predators. They have many predators or natural enemies. This would include wild **canids** (dogs, coyotes, and wolves). Bears and big cats (such as cougars, jaguars, and lynx) also hunt deer. Humans and automobiles take a large number of deer each year.[30]

The largest buck on record at present was a 47-point buck taken by a Tennessee hunter in 2016. The heaviest deer

---

[30] It is estimated that in the United States 42,000 deer are killed in collisions on the roads every year.

taken was reported to be approximately 540 lbs. (244.9 kg.) in 1977.

Some deer from some gene pool populations have a **recessive gene**[31] that produces a different coat color. One example is black deer, also called **melanistic** deer.[32] These are considered the *rarest of rare* and even more uncommon than the albino (white due to lack of pigment). In these deer, the gene causes the animal to produce too much pigment, known as **melanin**.

Deer sleep anywhere they bed (lay down) and may do so singly or in groups. Usually, deer will bed with their back to the wind. They are creatures of habitat, and they may bed in the same location day after day and month after month.

Dominant bucks have favorite bedding spots, and they will even kick subordinate bucks out. Deer seem to have mastered the ability to do most of their sleeping with their eyes open. And, when open, they sleep for only five

---

[31] Autosomal recessive genes (non-sex genes) do not show up in appearance in the offspring unless both parents carry that gene, and even then, there is only a 25% chance the offspring will show that trait.
[32] Melanistic - black or nearly black pigmentation

minutes or so at a time. Some reports indicated that deer take many "cat naps." during daylight hours. Regardless of whether awake or asleep, deer are continually monitoring everything going on around them. They are truly **timid** creatures, but they have an **elegant** mannerisms and style about them. *They are* **nature's timid but elegant** *mammals.*

REVIEW

1. How many different types of deer live in North America?

2. What are the two main and most common deer here?

3. Which North American deer is most common?

4. What is meant by *chewing the cud?*

5. Of the deer presented, which is the largest? Smallest?

6. What does photoperiod mean, and what does it have to do with antler growth?

7. What tends to be the most crucial factor in antler growth?

8. What happens to antlers that fall off?

9. When do fawns begin to lose their spots?

10. Which of these deer are endangered, and why do you think they have become so?

WHITE-TAIL DEER

COLORING PAGE

http://www.supercoloring.com/coloring-pages/two-white-tailed-deers

Name:_________________________

Deer: Nature's Timid but Elegant!

Carefully read each comment or statement. Write the correct letters to the answer in the proper boxes provided. Use the Word Bank if necessary.

eyeshine nourishment pronking Axis habit smell Fallow Cervidae stationary

mule beam fawns subspecies melatonin velvet edge key

Across

2. About 20-30% of these will die in a year's time

4. Exposure to sunlight reduces this?

7. Deer first introduced into Texas for hunting?

9. Deer see moving objects better than _______ ones.

11. Many of the deer in this book are thought to be _______.

12. Smallest of the real deer is the _______ deer.

13. Word used to describe the left and right main prominent antlers from which others grow..

14. An effect that causes and edge-adapted species

16. Closely related to tapetum lucidum?

Down

1. Deer escapees, probably from ranches?

3. Skin growing on new antlers?

5. Antler growth is mostly related to?

6. Sometimes hunters learn that deer are creatures of _______.

8. Form of deer trot?

10. Family from which all deer are from?

11. A deer will probably _______ you before it sees you.

15. The larger of the deer in this issue are the _______ deer.

INTERESTING SOURCES TO CONSIDER

A Deer Migration You Have to See to Believe. National Geographic. Available at: https://youtu.be/BIAyb-1uwTg

Axis Deer 101. Available at: https://www.youtube.com/watch?v=2MiwcYB7gDc

Baby Bear Tries to be Friends with Baby Deer. Available at: https://youtu.be/7I49oMXS_H0

Blacktail Deer In Rut. BIG BUCKS!. Available at: https://youtu.be/mQCAqBCKA2Y

Black-tailed Deer. Available at: https://youtu.be/6-JhQzqy9Yw

Buck Mule Deer in Yosemite National Park. Available at: https://youtu.be/YqtfoT2ewdM

Deer are Awesome: Whitetail Deer, Mule Deer, Blacktail Deer. Available at: https://youtu.be/qs-5CPdH8H0

Fallow Deer Facts: the Peter Pan of Deer, Animal Fact Files. Available at: https://youtu.be/Jf0Mf4Dmbm8

Fallow Deer Rut 2019. Available at: https://youtu.be/DEaXgAnpCig

Fallow Deer Rut: How to Call in Fallow Stag. Available at: https://youtu.be/GFkqqUXU6Ic

Giant Mule Deer Bucks on Antelope Island, Utah. Available at: https://youtu.be/DDMjqdVW7ZU

How Axis Deer are Impacting Parts of the United States. Available at: https://youtu.be/cNfYn-l0uyI

National Geographic Wild 2015: Private Life Of Deer | Animals Attack Wildlife Documentary. Available at: https://youtu.be/IVYkKci0BXY

National Key Deer Refuge. Art Loft 446 Episode. Available at: https://youtu.be/LrnpHF_Eheo

National Key Deer Refuge. Available at: https://bit.ly/2IHkjTm

Oh Deer! White-Tailed Deer Biology. Available at: https://youtu.be/q4UjWTNeTdU

The Albino Trailer. Blue Spider Production. Available at: https://youtu.be/plpCdo1Nxvg

Unbelievable wildlife Migration! Story of Wyoming's Mule Deer. Available at: https://youtu.be/5BcfnAJeHGc

White Fallow Deer September 2019. Available at: https://youtu.be/398j9hyKYcw

ABOUT THE AUTHOR

Richard NeSmith is a native of Florida, USA. He grew up wading through the swamps of central Florida with his two younger brothers during the pre-Disney era, and unknowingly, falling in love with biology, wildlife, and nature. He has lived in seven American states, twice in Australia and once in Mexico City. He holds eight university degrees and has taught for 14 years in secondary schools, here and abroad, and another 13 years as a professor in several American universities. His service includes professor of science education, Dean of Education, Campus Dean, as well as an online instructor. His passion for learning (and *how we learn*) did not develop until *after* graduating from high school. His only explanation for this is that *having a goal made all the difference in the world*. He enjoys reading, hiking, nature photography, golf, tennis, and RV camping.

http://richardnesmith.obior.cc

Applied **P**rinciples of **E**ducation & Learning *presents*

APE-Learning

AMAZON AUTHOR's PAGE:

https://www.amazon.com/author/richardnesmith

Educational, wildlife, and naturalist books
Dr. Richard NeSmith.

Issue 1
Raccoons:
Friendly Bandits
Dr. Richard NeSmith

Issue 2
Sandhill Cranes
&
Pileated Woodpeckers
Flaming Redheads
Dr. Richard NeSmith

Issue 3
American
Alligators
&
Crocodiles
Dr. Richard NeSmith

Issue 4
Bobcats:
Ghostly Elusive
Dr. Richard NeSmith

Issue 5
Foxes:
Sneaky Rascals
Dr. Richard NeSmith

Issue 6
Armadillo:
Little Armored One
Dr. Richard NeSmith

Issue 7
Squirrels:
Bushy Tail Scampers
Dr. Richard NeSmith

Issue 8
River Otters:
Aquatic Clowns!
Dr. Richard NeSmith

Issue 9
Beavers:
Nature's Engineers!
Dr. Richard NeSmith

Issue 10
Black Bears
Titans of the Forest
Dr. Richard NeSmith

Issue 11
Freshwater
Turtles
Dr. Richard NeSmith

Issue 12
FUNGI, LICHENS
& MUSHROOMS
Dr. Richard NeSmith

Paperbacks: http://amazon.com/author/richardnesmith

e-books: https://bit.ly/3iuCgB3

---

[i] **Special thanks to the following who kindly provided permission to use their photographs.**

From Pixabay: Raymond Cannon, suchitks48, Bishnu Sarangi, Mabel Ambe, TimZur, Joshua Choate and Gaby Stein.

Finally, *special thanks* to likeminded friends who love wildlife and who willingly shared their wonderful photos, and many of whom have become my friends: **Kerry Bowers, Stacey Diamond, Jackie Dibert, Karen Devins, Cindy Frasier**, and **Greg Jowers**.

Thank you everyone.

www.ingramcontent.com/pod-product-compliance
Lightning Source LLC
Chambersburg PA
CBHW040235240726
48664CB00001B/139